Flowing Expressions

Flowing Expressions

Author - Shreash Srivastava

Experience the thrill amid an ocean of emotions that the poet takes you through with each line and each word. Various colours of our lives painted in these texts.

Let's Begin :-)

Contents

What do they say about "Flowing Expressions" ?

A realistic potray of various human emotions through poetry. A commendable work!

Author Vishal Ved
Tomarkus & The betrayed Planet.

Endorsement by Vishal Ved - Author of bestselling science fiction novel on Amazon and world record holder book "Tomarkus and the Betrayed Planet"

श्रेयस के दिल की धड़कन

भारतेन्दु हरिश्चन्द्र ने कविता के संदर्भ में कहा था-

जामें रस किछु होत है,
ताहि पढ़त सब कोय।
भाव अनूठो चाहिए,
भाषा काहू होय।

अनूठे भावबोध का अहसास कराने वाले, संभावना से भरे कवि हैं श्रेयस श्रीवास्तव जिनकी अंग्रेजी कविताओं की सरसता सहज ही पाठक का ध्यान आकृष्ट कर लेती है।किशोर वय के इस संभावनाशील कवि को काव्य-कला अपने ख्यात पिता से विरासत में हासिल हुई है, मगर इस विरासत के खतरे भी कम नहीं हैं। सुखद स्थिति यह है कि इस कवि ने अपनी राह ख़ुद चुनी है और अंग्रेजी में अपनी अनुभूतियों को दिल से अभिव्यक्त करने का जोखिम उठाया है। सन् 2019 में पहला संग्रह 'माइ पोएट्री लेन' शीर्षक से छपकर चर्चा में रहा और अब कवि का यह दूसरा संग्रह ख़ास तौर से गौरतलब है। इन कविताओं से होकर गुजरते हुए एक ज़रूरी सवाल कौंधता है कि कवि के अंतस् में बेचैन छटपटाहट क्यों है? दरअसल यह कवि की गहरी संवेदनशीलता का द्योतक है।यही वजह है कि जब भी किसी घटना से कवि का सुकोमल हृदय उद्वेलित-आन्दोलित होता है, वह कविता रचने का दायित्व निभाता है, क्योंकि उसे पता है कि जो रचेगा, वही बचेगा।एक कविता में इस कवि ने अपनी रचना-प्रकिया अथवा आत्मकथ्य की ओर इशारा करते हुए कहा भी है कि सर्जना उसकी प्रेयसी है जिससे उसको बेइंतिहा प्यार है।विलियम वर्ड्सवर्थ का मानना था-'पोएट्री इज द इमेज ऑफ मैन एण्ड नेचर।' यानी, कविता मनुष्य व प्रकृति का शब्द-चित्र है।श्रेयस की कविताओं में एक तरफ उसका हृदय धड़कता है,वहीं दूसरी ओर परिवेश और प्रकृति के जीवंत चित्र भी अंकित हैं।अत्यंत सहजता और संप्रेषणीयता से बड़ी बात कहने की दक्षता इस कवि में उत्तरोत्तर पुष्पित-पल्लवित हो रही है, यह इसकी रचनाशीलता का शुभ संकेत है।आम तौर पर कहा जाता है कि मौजूदा दौर की युवा पीढ़ी साहित्य-संस्कृति से कटती जा रही है।मगर श्रेयस का अनवरत चिंतन व सृजन इस बनी-बनाई धारणा को ध्वस्त करता है।अपनी उम्र से कहीं अधिक के अनुभव और अनुभूति को काव्यात्मक अभिव्यक्ति का जरिया बनाने वाले प्यारे श्रेयस से अंग्रेजी कविता को ढेर सारी अपेक्षाएँ एवं आशाएँ हैं। इनकी कविताएं पाठकों की हर कसौटी पर खरी उतरें,यह मेरी दिली शुभकामनाएँ हैं।विश्वास है, संभावना से लबरेज़ किशोर कवि श्रेयस के इस अनुभूतिपरक कविता-संग्रह का स्वागत पूरी हार्दिकता के साथ होगा।

- भगवती प्रसाद द्विवेदी

Shreash's flowing expressions

Bhartendu Harishchandra said in the context of poetry -

The writing which has some juice to it,
Is the one which is read.
The expressions through words should be unique,
How does even language matter…

Shreash Srivastava, a poet full of possibilities, has a unique sense of emotion, whose succinctness of English poems easily attracts the attention of the reader. A talented young writer who has inherited such qualities in blood, but yet the dangers of this inheritance are no less. The pleasant situation is that this poet has chosen his own path and has taken the risk of expressing his feelings in English with all his heart. In 2019, the first collection titled 'My Poetry Lane' came out and now this second collection of the poet is especially significant. Reading through the poems, an important question arises: Why is there a sense of restlessness at the end of the poet ? In fact, it is indicative of the poet's deep sensitivity. That is why whenever the poet's heart is stirred by an event, he goes about penning down his lines, because he knows that the thoughts he writes down at that immediate moment will be the ones retained on paper and not lost amid other things. In one of the poems, the poet has also pointed to his process of creation or self-assertion and said that the art of writing is his beloved. William Wordsworth once said, "Poetry is the image of man and nature." That is, poetry is a depiction of man and nature. Shreash' poems on the one hand have his heart beating, and on the other hand, lively pictures of the surroundings and nature inscribed. The ability to speak greatly with utmost ease and communicability is progressively blossoming in the poet, which is a good sign of his creativity. It is generally said that the younger generation of the present era is being cut off from literature and culture. But Shreash' constant thinking and creation demolishes this supposed notion. English poetry has a lot of expectations and hopes from the talented Shreash, who has made the experiences and feelings of his age a means of poetic expression. May his poems stand every test of the readers, these are my best wishes. Confidently, this artistic poetry-collection of the potential laden teenage poet will be welcomed with utmost warmth and love.

- **Bhagwati Prasad Dwivedi**

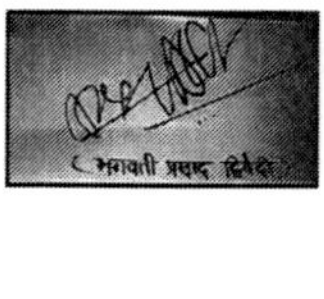

Art of Words

When it comes to poetry, it is definitely a reflection of the poet's heart and mind, because I believe that the field of creativity demands a passionate one !

The talented young Shreash's poems are an expression of his heart, a peek into its depths filled with an ocean of words. Knowing his talent personally, I can say that he has been able to manifest true, raw emotions and feelings through his creations... Congratulations and many many good wishes to him from the bottom of my heart !

Neerad (Cartoonist and writer)

Patna, April 14, 2022

जब कविता की बात होती है,
तो कवि के हृदय की बात अवश्य होती है...
क्योंकि मेरा मानना है कि
किसी रचनात्मक फसल की उपज क्षेत्र
रचनाकार का दिल होता है!
नवोदित कवि एवं युवा कवि श्रेयस
की कविताएं उसके दिल की अभिव्यक्ति हैं;
उसके हृदय की कंपन हैं और
शब्दों का महासागर है!
उसकी प्रतिभा को निजी तौर पर
जानते हुए कह सकता हूँ कि
वह अपनी रचनाओं से मानवीय मूल्यों,
भावनाओं को दिशा देनें में कामयाब
होंगे...
उन्हें बधाई व शुभकामनाएं बहुत सारी!
दिल से!

•

(नीरद, कार्टूनिस्ट व लेखक)
पटना, 14 अप्रैल, 2022.

PREFACE

I wrote this book just as its name expresses - that is whenever a thought, a line or phrase would come to my mind or I would be in a certain mood—be it happy, sad, upset, frustrated, charmed or whatever ; I just sat down and penned down my heart and feelings at that certain moment….these ideas and my pen just went in a flow - pure and raw.

Its been a long journey since my first book and I am pretty sure that you all will feel the same...we have come a long way in 3 years time.

Immerse your heart and mind as you go through these texts and see a mirror of relatable thoughts amid a vast space of versatile genres. Hope you love it :-)

I am really thankful to my family and all my loved ones who kept me going to compile this collection and bring it out in the best way possible . A special thanks to my mother **Shefali Srivastava** *- she's been the biggest support - always contributing in with her ideas and thoughts . Also to my father and elder sister - a big thank you .*

Special thanks to -

Bhagwati Prasad Dwivedi Ji *- It is an honour for me that I got such a beautiful foreword from him - One of the great writers of Indian literature .*

Neerad Ji *- His words of encouragement , transparent analysis of my work and his constant support - cannot thank him enough .*

Author Vishal Ved *- His mentorship and his guidance has been of immense value in this journey . A great friend and support to me :-)*

Mr. Abdul Razaq *- For designing such a beautiful cover and bringing out "flowing expressions" in an artistic manner .*

Thank you to everyone involved for making this collection a beautiful piece of art...

Dedicated to my mother,

for being my first cover designer

and giving me the best writing

motivation I've ever received :

" Rohan, keep going and finish

this book ; you will always fondly

remember this work of yours ^_^ "

Also a special mention to my

father and elder sister for being my

biggest cheerleaders .

Let the collection begin

"A Day in March never came so sweet" is the first poem that Shreash wrote on the themes of love and romance. A free verse poem which expresses youth, love and remembrance of innocent intricate feelings — common to everyone as an adolescent. The poem beautifully showcases the story of a selfless, true and compassionate bond which meets an unfortunate end.

Feel the connect of love and its connection to the month of March when flowers and love blossom.

A Day in March never came so sweet

A day in March never came so sweet,
I remember it as if it was our first meet.
Yes , we had been together since long,
Yet the truth is, that was the day it
Felt to me that we could actually tug along.
The very feel of her touch struck the right
chords , much above all my awards —
'n immediately did I whisper a quick prayer
to the almighty lords.

A day in March never came so sweet,
Flames and expressions of love —
Flowing through classmate sheets.
Not a moment without my girl,
She the proponent of dreams as clear as pearl.
That one name running in love,
Through the abyss of my youthful heart

A gunning dove — the only crew

In acting as a point dart.

A day in March never came so sweet,

In ways so fit that it will beat —

The memories of a past heartbreaking feat.

Yet now all seems disparingly incomplete

In love have I failed and fallen flat on defeat.

The wounds of a blurred past surfacing to convey the least, that I have fallen to deceit.

And now all that is left is a mind,

Reminiscing how a day in March had come so sweet.

For those who have loved someone with all their heart ...

"A writeup through the darkness with an open ended climax". Themes of uncertainty, fear, supposed bravery and courage are ingrained in the poem.

It highlights the thin line of difference between being courageous and ignorant and stupid. A tale "unfinished, untold" and yet containing imageries so bold ...

Amidst the Dark

The skies that cover a heartbroken lover,
Drops that strike the soil's cuffer.

They say he was his own perpetrator ,
An unlikely traitor — Tales still alive —-
Dictate the legendary navigator.

Yet "traitor" was the word hearing which,
His heart sank ; more on this later —
But his tale is worth a rank.

Yet amidst all this, he was surely lost and
damned.

" Wait, wait ! Don't take the bait. Prior to you
many set out on this unfortunate date"

Into the dark painful arc, a nasty hellish park.

And so and so, many and many more,
Such advises he received so as to not get deceived.
And amidst all this into the gloom he went.

As if to make a mark, unknown to all dangers
— That lurk, long way off into the dark.

Long drawn , carrying along, he stretched
and stretched - All broken and wretched.

In the ravine - all torn and devastated —
At that even a token of divine encouragement
was understated.

The moon's twilight — his countenance now
All pink and white — few wild berries for a
diet.

Amidst all this , there emerged the darkest of
sights — that big shadow finally steady ;
All gearing up to have his bite.

Unfinished, untold or so it is told.

And amidst all this, On the soil's cuffer —

A shattered soul was left to suffer.

*Experience the
uncertainty amidst the
dark...*

There are times when our mind just goes blank — tired and exhausted from the complications of our daily lives. We take so much pressure and stress due to various reasons — but forget about that mental exhaustion that our mind goes through.

Grinding ourselves each day, at times its better to keep the mind a blank slate, a thought which has been penned in this poem...

Times when the Mind is just a blank slate

Times when we are happy,

Times when we are sad.

Times when we are scrappy and

Times when we just go mad.

With so many happenings all around,

Our mind is fleeting lonely ground.

The roller coaster ride when it takes a toll,

Our mind plays the most important of role.

And so and so, many and many more

The exhaustion comes to the fore.

Finally the mind a spoiled bait,

Times when the mind is just a blank slate.

The next day, again on our own way,

Shuffling through life as we may.

The curiosity to know the good day,

And shine while the sun makes hay.

Everyone continuing in life's great race,

In a bid to outgun someone and be an ace.

Flavours of life, each presenting their own case,

Tasting each of them needs a lot of face.

Amid all of this, our mind loses its pace,

Yet the mortal man strives to keep his place.

More on this on a later date,

Times when the mind is just a blank slate.

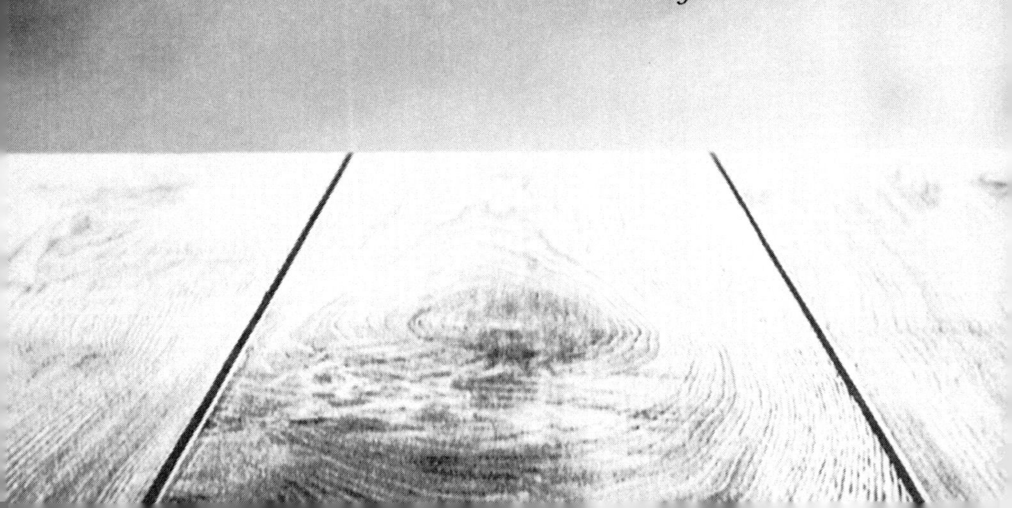

It's a long way to go , take it easy....

'The rare love of he', is a particularly open-ended poem that can have multiple interpretations, and the reader is free to explore. One such explanation could be that the poet describes the ideal friend that he believes doesn't exist per se but exists as his imagination, one that he still is on the lookout for. Sometimes when this bubble of imagination breaks, he finds himself as a loner and he must tread carefully on the journey until he finds 'him'.

Some interesting information : this poem is a very apt example of a hypophora, also referred to as an antipophora — a figure of speech in which the speaker poses a question and then answers the question.

The Rare Love of 'he'

Who is he ?

A rare gift is he, knowing no thrift is he.

A rare gift is he, who shares a bond of heart with me.

Shares a bond of heart with me, is always there for me.

Who is he ?

Someone whose friendship abounds in me, a rare gift is he.

A rare gift is he, whose love knows no bounds for me.

We talk , we make mess, we do play chess

We study with many a buddy, but I know he's my mighty best buddy.

Who is he ?

A rare gift is he, who can do anything for me.

Can do anything for me, such a precious gem is he.

Such is our bond that we both are fond —

Not of one but many similar things

And we often think, we have wings.

Who is he ?

A rare gift is he, the best of buddies is he,

A precious dream to me, rare gift is he.

I haven't yet found him, he is still in my dreams ;
I miss him in my team.

Hence, can he ever make way in my incomplete story ?

Till then I be very wary of a flatterer or
rather NOT such a precious 'he'.

We lack true friends and it's the biggest open secret. Flatterers are all around us — better to keep them at a distance.

The creation of each writeup has its own unique story behind it. " This world's against me ", is one such poem which has an interesting backdrop to it. The poet wrote this in a very personal space, in an upset mood at a time when he was drudging through a turbulent phase in his school and social life.

All that he penned down on one such sad afternoon, staring outside his window, came together as a piece of art, painted with an outburst of emotions enveloped by a melancholic heart and mind....

This world's against me

I am alone, only my soul is what I own.

They left me, even after promises of 'We'
that we'll be together even in a forlorn weather.

This world's against me, no one's with me.

Everyone thought, that I was a bot.

Didn't think of me as a human,
used me until my prowess was on the wane.

This world's against me, no one's with me.

My wish to be free, to gain liberty.

They didn't let me soar high,
clipped my wings when my destination was anigh.

This world's against me, no one's with me.

Now its only me , with a friend by the name of solitude.

I and my friend converse , even when everything's averse.
I gain courage although my aim is farfetched.

This world's against me, no one's with me.

I have learnt to brave storms
And even follow norms.

The word out there is that I'm down and out,
I have heard it now, my spirit's high,
And I'm ready for another bout.

This world's against me, no one's with me.

Realized that the world's cruel,
My fighting spirit is my jewel.

I am up, I am back - no one is for anyone,
Let them know this I owe no one.

The phoenix that I am has risen from the
ashes, won't have any clashes even if -

This world's against me, no one's with me.

A comeback is the greatest success story...

"Impulsive" - it's an interesting word. Meanings aplenty but the impulsive mind is what the poet talks here about. The poem explores the themes of anger, fluctuation of emotions and one's hasty and impatient attitude.

An impulsive person can at times be mistaken they say, deeds such which make him pay, yet many a times, " Impulsive as they say "...

Impulsive

Impulsive they say , anger
round the abstract bay.

That rush of adrenaline, followed
by release of Mr. Acetylcholine.

As the sensation grows on,
The con mind blasts on.

At first its just a loud call out,
Then it turns into a mis proud shout.

The mind plays its set of tricks to
Bind and slay the heart with impulse shrieks.

Gradually the impulsive attitude builds on
And unknowingly the offensive nature is far
from gone.

Anger is the word, which does
Lead to destruction unheard.

The words spelt out,
masked with those yells and shouts —

Do pierce the soft clear heart ;
When a fierce force oft tear it apart.

Impulsive is the word,
Making a person so often erred.

Well its seldom a peaceful stay,
drifting a person from his way.

The con mind yet as it may, after
many a sway - At last has the final say.

Well everyone has their own way,
Yet many a times, Impulsive as they say.

Being an impulsive
person could be
charming...

This is one short and witty poem, that Shreash wrote at a younger age, but has been included in this collection owing to its relevance for all ages. Exams and the vibes relating to it are never going to change for a student. Enjoy this light hearted poem and feel the joy and sorrows of examinations. Best of luck :-)

Oh ! Examinations

Exams ! Exams ! Exams ! Oh how they arrive,
And bring with them some anxious vibes.
Many subjects pour in a student's mind,
Excellent ones are one of a kind.

The pressure bundles up on a child,
Takes a toll even on an organised jay's mind.
Subjects vary from five to ten,
Ultimately some even go in vain.

From Mathematics to Algebra's antics.
From History's dates to Civic's fate.
From Geography maps to NCC caps.
From Grammar's fill in the gaps to Science hacks.

All round the year, the pressure cooks
In a student's head, at times even when in a cozy bed.
Exams are plenty , each one a unique testing entity.
Oh Exams ! Oh Exams !

Miss my pre class
X days :-)

'For another day' is a fresh retreat from the dramatic undertones of a lot of the other poems in the collection. It is fresh, playful and has romanticized the more trivial pleasures of life.

The major undertones are pastoral, romanticism, concrete visual poetry. Read the beautiful descriptive piece and feel yourselves being transcended to those spaces yourself. A lot of visual imageries and enveloped verses have been implemented.

For another day...

I have many stories and anecdotes to tell,
Incidents and happenings as well.

The view across the Marina Bay,
Or the beauty of the gulmohar flowers that lay.

Walking down that abstract way,
These will I keep for another day.

The scene of that rainy day,
When I saw those poor souls pray.

For they were stuck under the old tumble down hovel
amid May; and it was raining
Cats and dogs with lightning midway.

Driving through that foggy pathway,
These will I keep for another day.

The view from the top of Rohtang pass,
With the snow laden mountains stating all class.

The clouds hovering above the mighty mass,
Appearing just as its own crown glass.

The tourists from other shores —what they had to say,
These will I keep for another day.

Splashing the Beas's water in air,
Our whole group riding the swerving raft to dare.
Headgears and attires such we did wear,
Those experiences in those climes are golden ware.
Manali's traditional art's worth is beyond pricing to weigh,
These will I keep for another day.

Beautiful sights they all talk about,
Some myself I did mention here and thereabout.
But what of those views, which did at times make me
Doubt our hearts — where feelings of compassion are hard to sprout.
For the people and fellowbeings there on that way,
These will I keep for another day.

Visions and impassions they need to grow,
Broadening of people's mindset you know.
Methods and revolutions in fields that need to stay,
Revival of cultures and traditions that lay astray.

Upliftment of standard of living to flay,
These will I keep for another day.

Some good, some bad, some old, some gold;
Spectacles there are many more to see and behold.
Knowing that the world will grow a bit more bold
Such scenes need to be talked about and retold.
Joy, sorrow and moments of brilliance that slay,
These will I keep for another day.

Such extremes of visions we see, a change could be brought about by anyone — you or me :-)

An abstract poem which
has layers of expressions
and meanings to crack,
"Understanding my
challenge box", is a writeup
which tries to present an
individual's life, as a box
packed with challenges.

What's the fun in achieving
things that come easy,
accept challenges and do not
be sleazy and your
confidence should help you
sail through all breezy...

Understanding my challenge Box

Nobody understands me and yet I contemplate so,
Its only I who bear the brunt and lay deflate so.

They all give me suggestions, leaving my mind in
conjestion; it starts spiralling about,
Throwing mine own self in doubt.

I have many mouths here and thereabout
Some themselves a product of a lost bout.
And others struggling in there and their whereabouts.

All of their talks, a few mocks and
right then hit by a rock.

Such and such rocks, lie all around the docks.

The docks are my lengthened world,
Where well wishers are few and hidden in a curl.

In the shells and the highway up the docks,
There you find my challenge box.

Yes that box is spread and pebbled about so
In my fickle life or as they say so.

Times when I wonder about the wounded doe —
The one who surrendered itself to the hunter's footsteps-oh-oh.

In a nutshell, life is my challenge box I think so;
Not everything goes as we desire or like they say so.

The pebbles of life, or the wind that blows by,
Everything helps us grow and yet I contemplate so.

Don't limit your challenges ; challenge your limits...

Being insecure and feeling threatened by a better man or woman or feelings of inexplicable to ourselves is second nature to humans. But those who learn the tactics of surmounting this early on in their journey, have what it takes to reach the pinnacle of success. The poet explains well, how one should use focus on mitigating and using these insecurities to our advantage, in the hostile yet hopeful world that we live in.

Insecurities

Insecurity a word,
Leaving many dreams blurred.
Confidence becomes a third,
And often an unfortunate climax
Is there to be heard.

All of us have been insecure at different times,
A few in hard times, some in rattled mines
And a legendary few throughout their lifetimes.
But insecurity has worked up
its effect in all climes.

Consequences of this word is not a hidden fact,
Yet those a victim of it seemingly act.
Suffering themselves , with negative thoughts stacked,
Not seeking help even when
they are short on tact.

The world around us has become a lonely place,
Stories of such insecurity and unhappiness are
hard to brace.

Truth be told, if you are enough bold,
We live in a society which refrains from compassion
and love even when they are told.

Unfortunately the air around such cases is cold,
The modern society a place where emotions are sold.
It's a hard, lonely battle masked with obscurities,
For the one stuck in a tornado of insecurities.

Manoeuvring and self esteem among many a word,
Using which many problems can be permanently defrerred.
Confidence then gradually is multipled,
And a bright looking future is spurred.

Insecurities kill all things that are beautiful...

' Closer to your touch ' is a writeup that captures the essence and spirit of passionate love — story of young and blooming affections.

The fondness and feelings of compassion, the power of a 'loving touch' and adulation for one another has been highlighted through the magic of words in the poem. Feel the closeness and intimacy of youthful, teenage romance....

Closer to your touch

Amorous exchanges we did share,
When this longing heart had finally dared.

Desirous as much as it seemed,
You know how we did dream.

Passions which began as a love chance,
Are now irresistible without a daily glance.

Vibes - a lesser word as such but yet
It falls short to express how much
I felt closer to your touch.

At times standing a bit far , a few paces apart
Soaking in a charming heart of an adorable dart,
Admiring you - Thou a piece of art.

Others bearing an expertise in their craft,
Still yet fail to match up,
Their work to my beloved art.

Close as we are and closer much
With a daily dose of you as such
I felt closer to your touch.

The moments created together,
Wishes and prayers round a fluttering feather.

Words, times, memories and love,
Embedded in our ride full of crests and troughs.

Promises to be kept and miles to go,
Many chapters to add to this story you know,
Few differences to accept yet keeping up our bond so.

Your manner of holding my hands in a clutch,
Our impassions growing as much, it's clear
I felt closer to your touch.

Too often we underestimate the power of a loving touch...

The poem, 'My unnoticed pain' is written by the poet in a personal context, but in all honesty, it is an ode to all those young, inquisitional adolescents, who are casually denied the right to voice or even discuss their opinions by the apathetic responses from the grown-up club. The poet explains how this affects his thoughts and behaviour, and has taken to writing them down as a way to vent out all within.

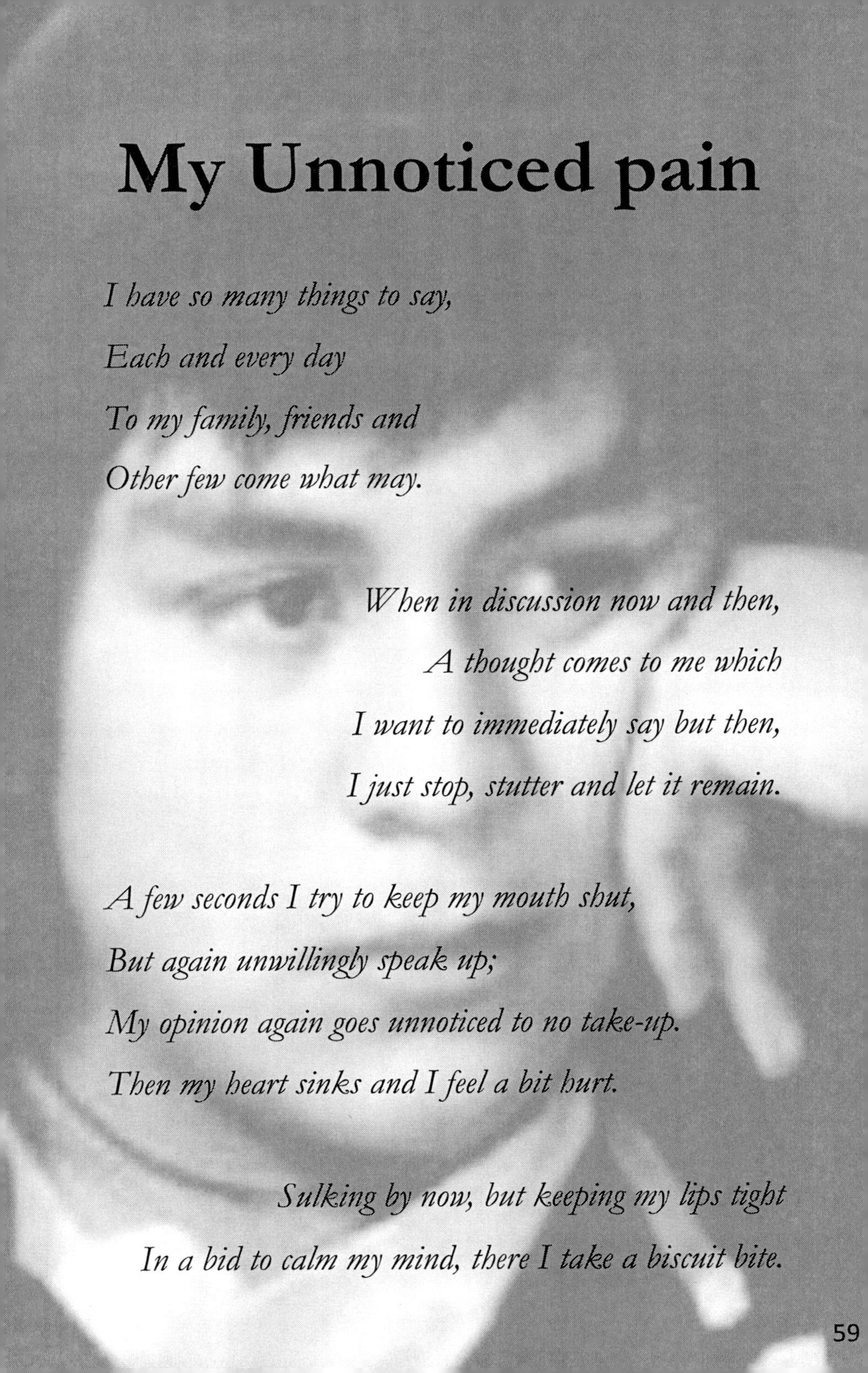

My Unnoticed pain

I have so many things to say,
Each and every day
To my family, friends and
Other few come what may.

When in discussion now and then,
A thought comes to me which
I want to immediately say but then,
I just stop, stutter and let it remain.

A few seconds I try to keep my mouth shut,
But again unwillingly speak up;
My opinion again goes unnoticed to no take-up.
Then my heart sinks and I feel a bit hurt.

Sulking by now, but keeping my lips tight
In a bid to calm my mind, there I take a biscuit bite.

Their discussions touching upon topics aplenty,

I forget my long drawn thought - all senti.

The opinion there dies down by now,

But who cares for this anyhow.

After the chit-chat comes to a close,

I go into my room with an upset pose.

All this while hurt with the unnoticed pain,

I pick up my pen, to let out those thoughts

I had sitting among other men.

To tell you these stanzas I wrote just then.

We all have experienced this unnoticed pain, haven't we ?

'Mister Alkenstein', might seem like a light-hearted, humorous poem at first glance, however, the beauty lies within the poet's ability to present deeper themes of the poem in an elusive manner and allow them to be revealed only to the wise reader. This style of poetry is called Burlesque, poetry that treats a serious subject as humour. Themes underlined in a darker tone are character traits like being overweening and self assertive to an extent of leading oneself to failure. Overall, the poet has successfully written a funny and witty poem to tickle your funny bone in a subtle manner, yet bring out a melancholic mood towards the end.

Mister Alkenstein

There lived Mister Alkenstein, lying in a tub of wine.

Always staying high, he lived on an island Tonga anigh.

His day started with a few "experiments of Alkenstein"

Usually which meant mixing different solutions with brine.

Brine was his favourite component, as his expertise on its solutions, had no formidable opponent.

Such solutions and mixtures he made,

That he had to wait on his luck's blade.

Menacing, vicious and fatal as much they were —

Alkenstein had survived 52 years in great fervour.

With each new mixture,
his "legacy" was a decided fixture.

Mister Alkenstein once visited the Rhine,

There he had his first taste of the famed red wine.

Back at the beaches of Tonga, one night fine

Something struck and he started to work his magic
On the solutions of brine.

Goodness, was this a sign ?

A sign of things to come-but all this while Mister Alkenstein
was soaked in rum ; his life now was all but glum.

All day and night engaged in his ground breaking project,
Most likely a wine making aspect.

Alkenstein wanted to make a wine - just as good as he had
tasted in the Rhine, determined to do that with his brine.

A year in making, Alkenstein had finally succeeded.

It was both — one which he ever so needed and one for
which even beggars pleaded — a dream had materialised
for Alkenstein — one which was seeded in the Rhine.

The next day he received deals and accreditation,

In celebration of which he threw
a big party for promotion.

....

Alas for Mister Alkenstein, unfortunately he was

But a sponge full of his own red wine — when a yesterday's
dealer knocked his door next morning at nine.

Mister Alkenstein was declared dead on the hospital bed —
With the doctors stating an overdose of a newly made wine.

All work and plans were shattered,
as was a competitor to the Rhine.

There lived one such Mister Alkenstein…

This poem is the first sonnet that Shreash wrote. An attempt to try a new writing style, led him to recounting his visit to the magnificent, famed Madame Tussauds of New Delhi.

The grand visions, the beautifully crafted wax statues and the ride of joy and happiness has been showcased through this poem — a first sonnet — weaving 14 lines of subtle mastery.

At Madame Tussauds

I arrived in Delhi not to have a look,

But to admire the attraction known as Madame Tussauds.

Since long having read about it in many a book,

There I was with my buddy squads.

We all were there soaking in the beauty of the waxy looks,

Designed and crafted by the master cooks.

Adored with the likes of Bollywood's Big B and King Khan,

To the God of cricket, his heir apparent and even a certain Jamaican superstar.

Icons such as Madonna and Hollywood's own Nicole Kidman,

Jennifer Lopez, Lady Gaga among others also on par.

Many moments and memories we did create,

Back on our flight talks and laughs about a certain star.

Those scenes were a piece of art to behold mate,

Such sights we clicked and witnessed on that day oh yaar.

Keep trying things at times, just like
I wrote a sonnet this time :-)

The poet has written this poem in a particularly pensive mood, lancing down the memory lane. The key themes of the poem are learning from the past, acting in the present and preparing for a brighter future assimilating all experiences and emotions from the chronicles of the past. Each stanza is an envelope verse — as the poet re-emphasizes on the mood and theme of nostalgia.

The poet recounts how he still loves to go back and reminisce the different flavours of his schooling and childhood days, in a very rhythmic fashion that doesn't feel heavy on the mind.

Nostalgic I feel so

We are always looking at the future,
Our goals and ambitions the inducer.
Use of past is something very subjective,
Depends on an individual's perspective.
Things we like to reminisce fondly,
And things which we dismiss promptly.
Incidents good or bad, help us grow,
Nostalgic I feel so.

A championship or a major winning,
First trophy or that good beginning ;
All those a source of confidence building,
These memories are all the while fulfilling.
A failure or a major disappointment,
Was also the backdrop of a comeback appointment.
Remembrance of those lessons to form that champion glow,
Nostalgic I feel so.

The many days spent in all those vibrant ways,
At that very place, which is today but an empty space.
How can I forget that childhood base,
Whose feel and look till today can I easily trace.
Old good friends when at times they meet by chance,
We still talk about our gully cricket's batting stance.
The Beyblade matches, games in those grassy patches,
Many other such talks arise in the flow,
Nostalgic I feel so.

A few incidents and visuals of my pre primary days,
The book fair, the pamphlets and excitement in our gaze,
Our talks, laughter's and innocent displays.
The friendship and rivalries of primary middle school days,
That energy and fire to set the world around us ablaze,
Remembrance of those carefree ways,
Still make me wonder and never fail to amaze.
That roller coaster school life we all undergo,
Nostalgic I feel so.

A lot of such unforgettable deep impressions,
Truths , lies , uncertainties and a few confessions.
Feel good remembering the past,
The ocean of emotions is otherwise quite vast.
The world we know, is evolving fast,
Staying in the present is very important to last.
Yet smiling at times and incidents years ago,
Nostalgic I feel so.

Some days I wish I could go back in life,
Not to change anything but to feel a few things twice.

‘ Dazzling Beauty ’, just as its name — has a particularly different mood, describing an abstract attire of 'beauty' that shines brighter than brightest of gems. With an inner light that captivates the mind and soul of the gazer.

A beautiful thing or person is an art, and art isn't supposed to be perfect, in fact it is supposed to make you feel something and thus there is no perfect definition to beauty, it is just a feeling described well by the poet.

Dazzling Beauty

Beauty - a fascinating word, but worth nothing
If the heart of the admirer isn't spurred.
A source of immense confidence for someone,
While a coarse competence for the kinda unlucky one.
The attribute is all but gloomy,
If one does not dazzle in the beauty.

Two facets of the same word —
Inner purity, that's the true beauty ;
And ravishing outer exquisiteness,
Which is all but refreshing dampness ;
And none of such hyped mediocrity,
If one does not dazzle in the beauty.

A quality worth its weight in gold,
But you know how is the story often told ;

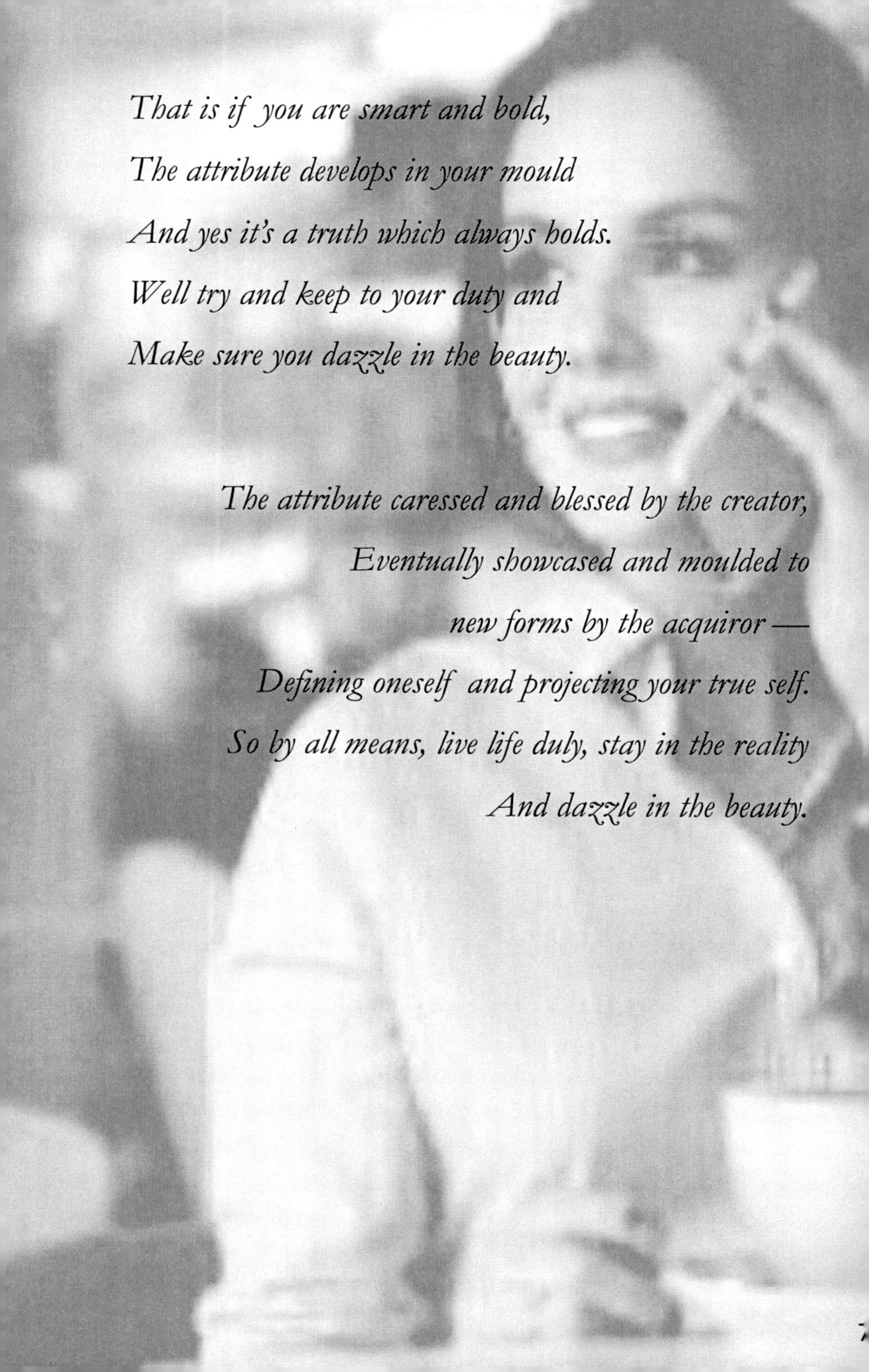

That is if you are smart and bold,
The attribute develops in your mould
And yes it's a truth which always holds.
Well try and keep to your duty and
Make sure you dazzle in the beauty.

The attribute caressed and blessed by the creator,
Eventually showcased and moulded to
new forms by the acquiror —
Defining oneself and projecting your true self.
So by all means, live life duly, stay in the reality
And dazzle in the beauty.

The seeds of beauty, are in humility...

'Few epigrams I state', a suggestive title indeed, for the style of poetry, implemented. An epigram is a very short, ironic and witty poem usually written as a brief couplet or quatrain. The term is derived from the Greek word 'epigramma' meaning inscription.

These short verses are short and impactful where words and lines have been used wittily.

Few Epigrams I state..

1

I'm tired of maintaining peace around me,
So many disturbances that I see
Makes it harder for me to let it be,
For pure silence is a writer's master key.

2

I love to convey my ideas about,
Feelings and expressions that sprout.
Penning them down without a shadow of doubt
New topics and flavours I like to scout.

3

Oh these sounds I hear,
Children screaming out of fear,
Seeing small assignments and deadlines near,
The naïve children oh dear.

Oh the world is but a stage,

People are here on a daily wage.

Time when they seem of no more use to the almighty sage, 4

He fires them and then they head to the death maze.

Yesterday by the coffee table I saw,

Young smart girls discussing the state law.

5 *Their personality and countenance without a flaw,*

So much so that they left quite a few gazing at them in awe.

Imaginations and dreams are free to go beyond,

Horizon and limits with the magic of a wand.

Not restricted around by the mind's bond, 6

We are our own favourite ever so fond.

Every epigram should resemble a bee ; It should have sting , honey and brevity...

'Its not hard to be right', is perfect example of a classical poetry style, villanelle (The villanelle, like the sonnet, is an old form with lots of rules. The good thing about writing a villanelle is that there's a lot of repetition, so once you have some of the lines chosen, you get to use them again and again. But making meaning out of that much repetition is challenging.)

Its a word of advice and wise thought, which dictates themes of righteousness and going back to the basics of being decently humane. The poet reinstates that it is never too hard to do the right thing, when one's intentions are clear and honest. The poem is an ode to reviving the good old virtues, ones which we are taught as kids and ones that we tend to forget as we grow older.

It's not hard to be right

It's not hard to be right,
Hesitation and fears aside ;
Pay heed and listen to that flickering inner light.

A few mortals wise enough know beyond common sight,
What lies past that horizon on the other side ;
It's not hard to be right.

The flaming Sun which shines all day so bright,
Even it knows when to go-leaving some darkness countrywide ;
Pay heed and listen to that flickering inner light.

And just like that it's better to leave at top of your height,
For otherwise you spoil someone's chances with the time you bide
It's not hard to be right.

Unfaithful , unclear and a store full of vice and spite,

People like these should be avoided than tried ;

Pay heed and listen to that flickering inner light.

Majority sing the same chorus as the world around every night,

It's risky you may think to swim against the tide,

but try once and you'll be your own pride ;

After all it's not hard to be right,

Pay heed and listen to that flickering inner light.

This time not any quote, it's the first villanelle I wrote...

In spite of the poet's burgeoning age, even he has his 'stories' to tell and has some mature advice for the readers and teens his age that he thinks has been fitting for him. The verses follow an alternate pattern of lines — the longer verses narrate while the shorter ones elaborate. Read this piece to gather some practical insights for your better sustenance in your personal and social spaces. The dramatic monologue lists out gems of the poet's very personal learnings that he wishes to share.

Convey you a piece of advice

Today I feel like spreading some knowledge,

Few things will I tell that someday even you will acknowledge.

A few thoughts and words to change your mindset,

Cut you some valuable treasured slice,

I want to convey you a piece of advice.

Through my 17 years of life,

I have gained some decent insight.

First being — that there will always be,

Such negative people around me

Who will only see the bad things in me.

If and ever such people pull you down,

Consider yourself a valuable crown.

"I'm the best" - thinking should make you feel nice,

I want to convey you a piece of advice.

Second on my list of invaluable insight,

[Well you can laugh on my confidence here, I won't mind]

Is that , staying positive all the time,

Even when you are not so fine, helps a great deal to be precise

I want to convey you a piece of advice.

A third thing which has helped me a lot,

When I'm busy sorting clouds of thought,

Is to be a calming self, with tried and tested methods

Which for you work well, take your time so that —

Your thoughts can gel - these things are of great help.

You must be wondering who am I that such things I tell,

Well, well it's just extraordinary situations I've dealt.

All those stories are worth a tale but for today's concise,

I want to convey you a piece of advice.

Fourthly , learn to be a bit more firm on your opinion,

Things you think and you counter are your own dominion.

Don't let strangers influence you, well wishers are often few.

Do things that feel good - add to your life some spice,

I want to convey you a piece of advice.

Last of all , the biggest gem you'll ever receive,
From a thoughtful teen like me to perceive ;
[Few lines more then I take your leave : ^)]
Criticisms and demotivating words you'll receive,
Forgetting and ignoring them is the best way up your sleeve.
Consistency in all things you do while at the batting crease,
Remember life wants to make out of you a masterpiece.
Such few lines I know will not suffice, yet
I want to convey you a piece of advice.

Don't cry because its over, smile because it happened ...

'Just before I write ' is one poem which is very close to the poet's heart. It has been kept as the last of this collection as it's a very apt one to end with, a poem in which Shreash tells everyone about just how he goes about writing a poem and what it means to him — his special love for literature and how his thoughts flow spontaneously. He has described in great detail all that goes through a writer's mind.

Read this monologue and experience the last of flowing expressions, as it leaves on you a lasting impression…

Just before I write

Every now and then whenever I get to write,
I try to relax, focus and be quite.
A few words, a few phrases seem to give a light,
But oh, the influx of thoughts is what I fright.
Then all that is left is a confused mind in plight.

I try to search for topics at times,
Within the world wide web's confines.
Seldom does this method succeed,
But when it does indeed, unfortunately few topics I like,
Which makes it harder for me to balance and strike.

Through the years what I have learnt of my writing style,
Is that whenever I imply my mood in awhile,
Taking it easy meanwhile and generating expressions
to compile, It's all worth the ultimate smile.
And yes at the same time I try to be as versatile.

Genres are aplenty, it all depends on my mood.
Classic novels and writeups I read - all day to them glued.
All of these give me some time to brood,
Over all that I need to prove,
And learn just how to get in the groove.

Last of all I want to say - Writing is love,
If you have a heart as clear as dove.
The passion is just never gone, a writer builds on
And creativity is there for everyone to spawn.
Right now walking down my lawn,
To be honest, such lines I wrote at the break of dawn.

*Didn't say it as well
as I might , these
things I do just
before I
write...*

If you loved the book , then please do consider leaving a **book review** *on the* **Amazon** *page :-)*

It will be of great help in reaching out to more readers and spreading the word about "Flowing Expressions" ...

...

You can follow me on Goodreads

Get to know me closely on my
Instagram handle - ***" me_shreash "***

Book available internationally in both
paperback and eBook forms :-)

THE END :-)

Until next time...

Created by Shreash Srivastava

Editing by Shreshy Srivastava

Designing by Shefali Srivastava

- Shreash Srivastava

I can personally attest to the fact that Quantum Physics has significantly contributed to a wide range of advancements in Molecular Biology and other areas of Biology in the modern age, bringing me much closer to a portion of this wonderful discipline.

I still clearly recall the day I was working on research on the ZIKA virus epidemic in India when I overheard a person talking to students and researchers on campus about the universe and politics, two equally improbable-sounding subjects. Even I needed a tea break, so I strolled outside and slowly joined the talks, which sparked a lively discussion that lasted for the following two days on campus.

The fact that someone could attract scholars from many backgrounds excited me. It took me no time at all to see that this man possessed an exceptional genius. It was Dev Arastu Panchariya and I encountered him as modest, kind, and alluring individual. He wasn't widely-known for his intellectual prowess at the time, but after listening to his original thoughts carefully on a range of areas for a few minutes, I was able to anticipate and even later approached to tell him that he would one day become an intellectual icon, which indeed he did become as an influential intellectual public figure. I'm proud and glad to have met him years ago, and every time we talk about something specific to discuss, it's as if I'm hearing him for the very first time. I absolutely see another Einstein or Socrates in him because of his totally distinct attitude and approach of thoughts to not only science but to everything else and that what makes him differ than rest of us.

I highly commend this book to everybody and everyone who is interested in reading something truly momentous. I am grateful to Dev Arastu for producing this excellent literature, which will definitely achieve its goal of spreading profound wisdom across humankind.

I express my best wishes for his future avenues !

Bhuvanesh S. Kalal, PhD

Alumni, Wayne State University, USA

Researcher, Molecular Biology

University of Kentucky, USA

I was first introduced to Mr. Dev Arastu Panchariya in the Hon'ble Parliament of India, couple of years ago. At very first instance, I found Dev Arastu to be a very humble and enormously gifted person in so many ways, with captivating interactive abilities as a Philosopher of highest order. It was evident that he was going to do great wonders with his creativity, and that he would surely dignify the Indian fate in history as one of the most original thinkers both as a culture in world and country. He exactly fits by his name "Arastu" which refers to "Aristotle".

His humble background and charisma connected with grounds have certainly evolved him silently. It is the gifted state which prepares an individual to get ready for the toughness of life, and the key observations for everything finally constructs a formidable creature. Dev Arastu is also a historical part of this process. He has a unique ability to think through philosophy and rationality. His ability to think and then integrate makes him different from others. The best part of Dev Arastu is that he understands what he understands and he truly believes every word he says. That matters most for anybody in life and I never seen this quality ever in my long spanned career.

I am delighted that he is inspiring by his great work, revolutionary ideas, Polymathic and leadership personality. But for me, his humility has remained everything. The brilliance loses its colour if it ignores the basic constructs of a good human being.

I wish good luck to Dev Arastu for his great book that will create a genuine interest among ordinary people to read and become great pathfinders of curiosity in their lives. I hope to see more Dev Arastus in all parts of India and in every century and era across the globe, and to make it happen this book will be the first and foremost step because he, himself, is a true inspiration and that's why his every legendary word contained by the book will propagate more inspiration thoroughly.

Best wishes,

Dr. Nanditesh Nilay

Alumni - Indian Institute of Technology (IIT), Delhi

Fellow - ICSSR

Author and Faculty

(Philosophy & Ethics)

HESTEN
an Imprint of BlueRose Publishers

My first meeting with Mr. Dev Arastu Panchariya was an impressive one and indeed a lifetime of an experience. I was mightily impressed by this fine example of a human being who seemed like an open Pandora's box full of universal knowledge and a kind of wisdom that can never be expressed in mere words. His love and penetration in a wide range of fields like Theoretical Physics, Cosmology, Mathematics, Economics, and extremely fascinating Philosophy was evident in the way he spoke about it and the way his eyes lit up every time he dwelled deep into all these areas of rare depths. While holding a gifted proficiency over deepest technicalities, his erudition even to communicate everything is also very much admirable which I felt in order to explain it to a common man like me. At the end of our session, I discovered a new found respect not just for all those glorious fields mentioned above, but also for this wonderful, intuitive and extraordinary Genius person - Mr. Dev Arastu Panchariya. At the same time, his seniority as a personality in life and accomplishments in all these fields are such heroic that I feel so honored and proud from both the side of me as a person and the entire Hesten Publication House [A Traditional Imprint of Bluerose Publishers], to be a part of this book greatly written on "Quantum Physics" which has also been a personal curiosity for me. The best I can say in my limited capacities of words, after having read the wonderful Book, is that the inscribed literature by him is not a Book, but "The Legacy".

Best Regards

Syed Arshad

Director

To Be Continue...